Rockstar Business

Adii Rockstar

Dedication

I'd like to dedicate this book to:
My dad, for teaching me about business from a very young age;
My mom, for showing me that life is about people; and
My beautiful fiance, for reminding me of the happiness I derive
from my job.

Contents

Prologue   1

Chapter 1: Introduction and Definitions   **2**
    Introduction   3
    Rockstar what!?   5
    Tailor-made for business   6
    Bye bye traditional   7
    Enter the Entrepreneurial Rockstar 8
    Know your Reasons   9

Chapter 2: Evolution   **10**
    Becoming more   11
    Staying true to yourself   13
    The Trust Challenge   14
    Ambition is hard work   16
    Passion is easy   18
    Be Addicted   20
    Motivation via Challenge   21
    Become a visionary   23
    Goal-setting and Idealism   25
    It's in your hands   27

Chapter 3: Decisions and Values   **28**
    Acting the part   29
    Rogue-starness   30
    Defying the black-and-White   31
    Be Impulsive   32
    Don't get caught in the details   33
    Your Risk Boundaries   34
    Make Mistakes   35

Being Trustworthy   36
Business isn't just always Business   38
Transparent Success   39
It's never about the money   41

Chapter 4: Spend time outside your own hype   **43**
The Challenge   44
Rockstar Inspiration   45
Inspirational Interactions   46
Online is over-rated   48
Roots and Hobbies   50

Chapter 5: Branding   **52**
You are the Brand   53
Personal vs Business Branding   55
Be Yourself   57
Personal Responsiveness   58
Don't stereotype yourself   59
Make time for Others   60
Nobody is Bigger than You   62
Whorestar   63
Being the Expert   64
Branding in Practice   67

Chapter 6: The Business   **69**
6.1: The Team   70
Business is about People   71
Surrounding yourself with great people   73
Picking your team   75
Culture   78
Getting help from the start   80
Sharing wealth and incentives   83
Taking a Personal Interest   85

Never limit Anyone or Anything   87
Creativity at all costs   89

6.2: The Ideas   91
The Planning Stage   92
Out of the Box   94
Be Vigilent   97
Ignore the competition   99
Balancing Contingencies   101
Picking the Right Idea   103

6.3: Running the Business(Model)   105
Build Something   106
Organic Growth   108
One Way Only - Add Value   111
Cash Flows, Financing and Wasting Money   113
Who's money to risk   115
Diversification and Sustainability   117
Checks and Balances   120

Chapter 7: Conclusion   **122**

Prologue

My name is Adriaan Pienaar, I'm 25-years-old and if you're reading this book, I suppose you consider me to be pretty successful. I have an Honours degree in Business Strategy and Management but I've only ever applied it (directly anyway) during a 2-month stint when I was employed full-time at a corporate company. For the rest of my time, I've been building businesses…

Until now, my fascination with building businesses has spawned three different projects: WooThemes, which I co-founded in 2008; radiiate, which I first launched in 2007; and, most recently, The Rockstar Foundation, which brings balance to the otherwise capitalist approach to my business life.

In Rockstar Business, I will draw on the experience and knowledge that I have gained from each of these projects* and reflect upon the last couple of years of my life.

* Whilst WooThemes has been my most significant success (and the one that has inspired me to write a book entitled Rockstar Business), I have specifically chosen to not reference it in this book. Along with my two Woo co-founders, Magnus and Mark, we are working on a book that will specifically discuss WooThemes in great depth; thus I have dedicated all Woo-related matters to that future book instead.

1 Introduction and Definitions

Introduction
Rockstar what!?
Tailor-made for business
Bye bye traditional
Enter the Entrepreneurial Rockstar
Know your Reasons

Introduction

Reflecting on who you are and why you've been (relatively) successful isn't a task for the faint-hearted, as I've discovered whilst writing this book. When you're focused on working away at the challenges, ideas and dreams that consume your days, you tend to not really notice your surroundings, the reasons for your specific actions or the consequences of the impulsive decisions you make.

There is, however, a problem with that approach: when you've become a supposed "master" at marketing yourself, you tend to start believing your own hype. The trick to overcome this problem is to cut through the self-imposed clutter, and, for me, to figure out what exactly has made me tick and allowed me to market myself as a Rockstar (you'd think that there'd be at least some truth to it if you look at the evidence).

Rockstar Business is an analytical - and hopefully an inspirational - look at how I've turned myself into a self-branded Rockstar.

This book is a collection of inspirational stories and thought-provoking reflections that I have discovered across my journeys of the last year. If I told you that I had empirical evidence to back up any of my claims, I'd be lying. However, I do believe that my business achievements to date are sufficient proof that I'm doing at least something right, and that, at a minimum, you could be able to learn from and evaluate my face-value thoughts. The most important thing to consider is that I don't believe that there is a right or wrong here; but that everything I say in Rockstar Business has worked for me. Most importantly, it's been successful for me because I made my business ventures fit uniquely to my personality, my goals and my methods of acting on trusted impulses.

Rockstar Business might not seem to work right for you: that's because you will need to adapt my approaches and their implementation to your life and your work in a uniquely "you" kind of way.

My Rockstar brand is entirely self-created and whilst I've been successful enough to create some hype around that, I'm not an international celebrity or worth multiple millions. Instead, I'm a 25-year-old entrepreneur and I've been lucky enough to draw my own canvas; and it is within that space that I've found immense inspiration, self-confidence and extreme happiness. In this book, I would like to share what I've learned with the hope that you too can find the inspiration, self-confidence and happiness that I associate to being a Rockstar.

With that said, if you're looking for a "How-To-Be-Successful," "Make-Millions," "Work-Only-4-Hours-A-Week" type of book, then you need to look again, because Rockstar Business isn't that. I don't have any rules or 3-step plans which will guarantee success, because I don't believe that following and copying someone else can make you successful.

Ultimately, no one reading this book will find success in attempting to become "Adii Rockstar". However, if you take the ideas and inspiration presented in Rockstar Business and implement those in your own unique ways, you will be a little closer - or even better - at running your own Rockstar Business.

Rockstar What!?

To get started, I need to explain my ideas behind the "rockstar" term.

Before I started to brand myself as Adii Rockstar, I didn't really have a brandable identity. My birth name, Adriaan Pienaar, just doesn't shout entrepreneur or rockstar in any way. So when the definition of a rockstar popped up in a conversation with a friend, I immediately felt that I could relate to the ideas behind the term and concept. More importantly though, I was able to take a seemingly generic term and really make it my own.

To me, being a rockstar represents finding an identity within oneself, which aligns with one's preferences; personality traits (the good and bad, strengths and weaknesses); as well as the goals, dreams and ideas for one's life going forward.

My definition of "rockstar" thus needs to be different from yours, because if we had the same definition, it would only be successful for one of us. The definition and subsequent identity is also not in the word itself, but instead in that identity that we create around the concept. So, you could replace "rockstar" with whatever floats your boat, as long as you find that identity that will challenge you, fuel your growth and vitality going forward and create happiness in your surroundings.

Tailor-Made for Business

"Rockstar" is a generic term and your personal connotations with the term should include references to all the different spheres of your life. Since business is one of my biggest passions, it is within that space that I've found the most appropriate use for the implementation of a Rockstar brand and identity.

The reason for this is that a lot of my thoughts and opinions have been greatly influenced by popular marketing and branding principles, which have been in practice for ages now. With Rockstar Business, I have attempted to implement those in a slightly different way, where the brand itself (in this case, you!) benefits from being a brand, being exposed and marketed to your audience. Whereas traditional marketing approaches focus on the "outward" flow, I'd like to think that by identifying myself as Adii Rockstar, I've created for myself a maintainable source of positive inspiration and energy (an "inflow" generated by the Rockstar brand).

Another reason can be found in the definition of being an entrepreneur, considering that being an entrepreneur is not far off from this book's definition for being a "Rockstar." Both of these concepts will share quite a few characteristics of successful entrepreneurship. If you were to put an entrepreneur & a Rockstar side-by-side, they'd make very similar decisions.

The Rockstar does, however, have an edge over the entrepreneur, as its identity is more evolved and much less stuck in "yesterday's ways of going about your business".

Bye Bye Traditional

The playing field has changed. The player—and the definition of that player—needs to evolve.

Presently, Successful Entrepreneurs are defined as:

- People that identify gaps within markets;
- People with a high-risk appetite to fill those gaps (and subsequently profit from their efforts);
- People perceived to be highly educated;
- People who started and ran their own businesses that have subsequently turned into business empires.

These characteristics aren't as relevant or applicable as they were in the past. This is (mainly) due to the fact that the business landscape in which we operate has changed considerably; it continues to change on a daily basis.

The "Successful Entrepreneur" has become a passé business label, a hall pass to use in the corporate jungle.

We desperately need a concept revolution; a new idea—a definition and application that stands for more than "Successful Entrepreneur."

Enter the Entrepreneurial Rockstar

The new, modern entrepreneur works smart fewer well-spent hours resulting in (increased) success. Yes, it is possible; it just requires a mindset shift.

An Entrepreneurial Rockstar's happiness doesn't rely solely on financial success. Wealth, from a lifestyle perspective, is highly valued.

Rockstar Entrepreneurship offers a holistic approach to business. These cutting-edge entrepreneurs invest a greater portion of time and energy in pursuing and maintaining personal happiness this is in addition to their focus on business deadlines and the bottom-line.

These modern entrepreneurs favour a collaborative approach; they work and surround themselves with the best people. With this strategy in place, the entrepreneurial focus shifts from being "the only" to being "one of." Relationships are prized and interactions are not valued solely by existing or potential monetary worth. In its simplest form, being an Entrepreneurial Rockstar is less about the wallet and more about the soul.

Know Your Reasons

Before we embark on the rest of the journey within this book, I need to explain that being a Rockstar is not about money, greed, over-indulgence or finding a quick way to be superficially happier and more successful. If any of those things currently contribute to your motivation for reading this book, then you are most probably going to be disappointed.

During the rest of the book I will elaborate on topics that include staying true to your inner-self, being honest and transparent and, irrespective of any branding, to act and be yourself. You are likely to realize that if your motivations aren't aligned with these principles, you're going to struggle to find much value in my way of thinking.

Being a Rockstar is dependent on you being you, because the very essence of becoming a Rockstar is about taking your uniqueness and just moulding it into something that is more accessible, more brandable, and more content (on a personal level), all of which will ultimately lead to more success and a sustained happiness.

Before you possibly waste your time thinking that Rockstar Business will help you nurture only superficial desires, I invite you to ensure that your reasons taking this journey to Rockstardom are indeed viable and include achieving a meaningful happiness. Being a Rockstar is about self-fulfillment on a higher level—and from personal experience, money and success have no influence on those upper echelons of our personal well-being.

Evolution

Becoming more
Staying true to yourself
The Trust Challenge
Ambition is hard work
Passion is easy
Be Addicted
Motivation via Challenge
Become a visionary
Goal-setting and Idealism
It's in your hands

Becoming More

Rockstars operate on a higher playing field; a place where most ordinary people tend not to wander and wherein the context of your thoughts makes much more sense than it would in real life. This may sound slightly like those "Pie-in-the-Sky," "How-to-be-Happier / Richer / More-Successful" theories, but the truth is that only you are able to dictate those measures in your own world and life.

I've found that being within touching distance of your own psyche and personality allows your mind to operate within a space that is secluded to the rest of the world. Within that space, the world's average rules, theories and requirements don't seem to matter as much, because all that matters is your own happiness, your ambitions and your ideas.

This isn't meant to be an egotistical approach to living your life, either; instead it's about understanding who you are. Once you have that primal understanding of yourself as a person, you will be better able to understand your place within the context of the real world. Furthermore, I'm not suggesting some kind of rat-race towards finding your personal zen, but I do believe that it is extremely important to understand your personality, soul and unique characteristics (both the benefits and limitations thereof).

By now, you should have a good understanding of what it means to be a Rockstar, but within this section I would like you to shift that understanding to the side and focus on only one thing: yourself. Without starting a meditation session or taking up yoga, I'd just like to explore some key personal considerations with you. These will ultimately influence your own roadmap to becoming a Rockstar and being involved in a Rockstar Business.

As I mentioned earlier, I can pitch many great Rockstar-like ideas your way in this book, but if you pursue and implement them as I would, then you wouldn't be any nearer to their success. Instead, you have to take those ideas as building blocks and fuse them together with your own unique personality. On that premise, I'm willing the bet the price of this book that if you allow yourself to undertake this journey with me, you will be closer to being a Rockstar in your own right.

Staying True to Yourself

The most important thing that I can tell you in this book is this: Always stay true to yourself. Always.

Too many people tend to get caught up in the hype and promises of inspirational how-to books, but only end up trying to emulate someone else's success. Irrespective of anything that I tell you within Rockstar Business, you need to make sure that you never sell your soul, because being a Rockstar is dependent on you being yourself and harnessing your own unique attributes in such a way as to achieve happiness and success.

This is also important if you consider that you will only be successful in spaces that you can relate to personally. A little bit later in this book we'll explore passion and an addiction towards this Rockstar journey, but for now, you need to understand that the only way for you to be passionate and addicted to anything is if that appeals to your psyche and personality.

Trying to base this journey on false pretenses would be futile and I can't see how anyone would be able to sustain such superficial motivations. Make decisions (for your road ahead) based on who you already are as a person; whilst we can refine and build on that, we will never steer too far from what you've already got.

The Trust Challenge

Trust is most probably one of the biggest challenges within our daily lives, not only in the professional spheres, but all over. The reason for that is purely that in every single sphere of our lves, we are surrounded by other people. Thus, the need to trust in some people is completely unavoidable.

The problem with trust, however, is that most of us have lived through bad experiences where our trust in others had been compromised. This means we tend to be over-cautious in terms of who, when and how we trust, when instead we should recognize the positive influence trust can have on a business.

Start trusting yourself

For Rockstars, the first step is to trust yourself because if you can't even keep that going, you'll have a hard time trusting in other people. Trust your ideas, your vision, your way of doing things and most importantly, trust your common sense about other people. Trusting yourself is the foundation upon which you make decisions about whom and what you are supposed to trust outside of yourself.

To an extent, trusting yourself is a self-confidence thing, because the more you experience the positive effects of trusting yourself, the more confident you'll be in placing more trust in your own abilities and personality. The secret is to force your way into that mindset, which will allow you to fuel your Rockstar confidence and trust.

The end-result is an exponential cycle where self-confidence breeds self-trust and the success from that breeds more self-confidence.

Trusting others

Once you understand that you need to trust yourself, you need to learn that it is similarly important for Rockstars to trust in others.

I can tell you now that not trusting those around you can be the biggest drain on our time because we end up taking care of everything ourselves. Not only does this limit our time, but it also limits our productivity and capacity we risk missing out on new opportunities that may come our way.

Business is no fun and just ain't worthwhile if you can't surround yourself with people you can trust. These people could be business partners, team members or mentors. Irrespective of their roles in your business, they still need to be there and you need to be able to trust them.

Relying on yourself to be solely responsible for running your business is a futile exercise and not very Rockstar at all.

Ambition is hard work

As a youngster, my parents always encouraged me to be ambitious in everything that I attempted in life, so to say that this kind of thinking has been ingrained in my life would be an immense understatement. Nevertheless, as I've grown older and hopefully more mature, I've learned that ambition comes packaged with one major proviso: it's a heck of a lot of hard work.

See, it's fine to be extremely ambitious (as every Rockstar should be), but most people will fail at their ambitious journey to Rockstardom if they fail to work extremely hard at attaining those dreams and goals. That should've already been quite obvious to most of you; nobody gets anywhere in life without the hard work. What I meant to say, though, is that ambition in itself is hard workalmost to the extent that it becomes a curse.

I'm an incredibly ambitious person (this book being evidence of that) and a lot of my ambitions tend to not be overly realistic. But thankfully, many of them are very achievable too, so I'm pretty much left spending my work time chasing down these ambitions in one way or another. Because I'm naturally so driven to achieve these dreams and goals, I really only have one way to be successful and that's to continue working hard and for the sake of satisfying that ambition.

The down side to ambition is that ambitious people tend to not be able to shut down completely or just stop having new great ideas that they want to pursue. It can be difficult for ambitious people to be content during those times that require not working very hard within their pursuits. I would also like to think that ambition and willingness to work harder than anyone else is part of a Rockstar's required make-up.

Ambition and hard work go hand-in-hand for Rockstars. The only way to satisfy this inherent, natural hunger is to throw everything you have into that pursuit.

Passion is easy

All this talk about the difficult and strenuous nature of pursuing your dreams and passions can become somewhat negative after a while. Nevertheless, the fact remains that when you love what you do, it tends not to feel like work. And besides, the only way to truly love your daily obligations is to be totally passionate about them (whether a 9-to-5 job or your own projects and ventures).

Even better is that passion is really easy to muster because it is already within you, you just need to identify the areas in your life that inspire that passion for something. Passion can be found in so many areas of life, but if you are able to identify the things that get you really excited about working hard, then half of your journey is already completed.

The first place you should look for passion is within your hobbies and interests. The stuff that keeps you busy (outside of work-time) tends to be the stuff that appeals to you the most, and I'd bet that within that collection of hobbies and interests you'll find a few subjects that make you truly passionate.

You should also spend some time understanding the less obvious and less tangible things that get you into a passionate mood. On my journey to Rockstardom, I've come to realize how various challenges get totally psyched up, I have an incredible passion for completing a good challenge (more on this later). For you, it could really be a variety of secondary subjects or interests that are, again, totally specific to your own personality and character. And remember, it's worthwhile exploring the things that make you happy and make you feel positive because you'll better understand the things you are passionate about.

Once you have identified the things that you are extremely passionate about, you need to begin cultivating those passions by way of implementing your passions in your daily life. If you are passionate about cars, then figure out how you can learn more about cars and grow that knowledge to the level where you may be able to create a new business model and potentially plug a gap in a related market.

The unspoken key here, however, is to actually give yourself time to explore your passions, as good ideas will definitely sprout from your "addiction" to what you're most passionate about. Focus on fueling your passions. As they grow, you will begin to discover and focus on new ideas while cutting out unnecessary clutter from your life.

Be Addicted

Addictions get such a bad rep these days, but I would venture to say that an addiction to the right kind of things (like your passions) and the ability to balance that addiction marks a true Rockstar.

Looking at myself and what I've learned and experienced on my journey as an entrepreneur, I can easily point to a few things that have me totally addicted. What are they? Simple stuff like being loyal and transparent, being genuine (as far as possible) in all my interactions, working very hard, but finding a balance between work and play, and so forth.

If those attributes are generally considered as "good (Rockstar) attributes," then why would an addiction in this regard necessarily be bad?

I think it comes down to focusing on the "right" subjects in life and then valuing those ideas, issues and factors that contribute most to the betterment of your life, your business and your environment. The details of your positive addictions will certainly differ from one Rockstar to the next. Nevertheless, they are inevitable characteristics of Rockstars, and outside observers tend to associate things like positive addictions to men and women of good and productive social standing.

By focusing on passions and positive addictions - and fueling your addictions to get even better at implementing those in your life - you begin to have a clear, yet modest, view of your life going forward. Greed, arrogance and ignorance kind of fall by the wayside because they are pushed out by one's addiction to the good things in life, thus minimizing the risk that you're missing the whole point of being a Rockstar.

Motivation via Challenge

Rockstars love challenges because they are ultimately the best and easiest way to motivate oneself.

I love a challenge, over and beyond any other reason to chase a goal or dream. I'm enthralled by building businesses not because money, success or financial freedom are my primary goals (those are goals too, but secondary goals), but instead because I want to prove that I'm good enough to accomplish the challenge of creating a business. It may sound like I'm simply playing with words and that I'm just a greedy capitalist like the rest, but I believe there is a blessing in this approach.

When you motivate yourself to work towards certain goals and dreams, what becomes most important is your focus, in terms of your planned roadmap to success and accomplishment. It would be easy to motivate yourself with superficial needs like money and perceived public success. But problems ensue when you lack progress on those artificial fronts: they don't seem to be sustainable. Instead, approach any goal or dream more holistically and motivate yourself through "organic" or natural means, like striving to succeed the challenge and harnessing a feeling of self-fulfillment (these needs are already be present within your make-up, so it simply becomes a case of harnessing the desire for self-fulfillment in an actionable form).

The added benefit of using challenges as your primary source of motivation is that other people's cynicism and disbelieve in your goals and dreams give you tons of motivation. When other people tell you "You're never gonna make a success of X," or, "It's impossible for you to create a business selling Y," you've suddenly be granted the easiest way ever to motivate yourself. The approach of harnessing defiance as motivation is almost like be-ing the underdog in a big sports match: you are on your own and nobody thinks that you will be able to achieve your goals.

Never underestimate the power of being challenged to outperform other people's perceptions. Allow others' lack of confidence in you to fuel your motivation and go full-tilt at knocking down one challenge after the other.

Become a Visionary

I don't really believe in being born with a silver spoon in one's mouth. Some people are naturally more talented than others, but hard work will generally get you much further in life than having natural talent.

In other words, anyone can learn most of the same skills that you would attribute to your average, successful entrepreneur.

One of the skills that I'd associate with most Rockstar entrepreneurs is the ability to be a visionary in terms of the strategies, processes and ideas that are implemented within their businesses. In a world where most problems have already been solved, it is essential to be unique and creative in terms of the products and services that one provides to consumers.

The only way to achieve that level of uniqueness and creativity is through being able to have a vision of where the business should be going in future (and then making your business decisions accordingly).

Getting back to the point I made at the beginning of Rockstar Business: I don't necessarily think that all Rockstar entrepreneurs are born as visionaries. If I take myself as an example, I definitely don't consider myself a visionary, even though I have been able to make sound decisions now (based on a future idea or vision) that have turned out to be great down the line.

The trick is to allow yourself to be a visionary by allowing yourself to dream.

I find that a lot of people have a lot of great ideas, but they somehow tend to limit those ideas (in terms of never pursuing them), because they become "realistic" (and negative) before they have even had the opportunity to flesh out those ideas.

Most of the future-defining ideas that have been concocted by true visionaries weren't very realistic at first. Just because some ideas don't seem practical at first shouldn't prevent you from exploring them in more detail. I believe that every successful entrepreneur is also a dreamer at heart, which means that every one of us should also be able to be a visionary. I also believe that every great business has been built on a dream.

Allow yourself to dream. Allow yourself to be creative and more importantly, allow yourself to become a visionary. It only takes one Rockstar idea to turn into a successful business to convince others that you are indeed a true visionary.

Goal-Setting & Idealism

So far, we've discussed the importance of figuring out who you are, how to discover your passions, and that if you become totally addicted to those passions, you can formulate visionary ideas. The next step toward Rockstardom is to set goals for yourself. Instead of doing this in the traditional way (where all goals need to be specific, measurable, achievable, relevant and time-based), I'd like to suggest a more Rockstar approach to creating and setting goals.

I have realized that life and its ambitions are less about the attainable and measurable goals and more about challenging oneself, one's views and dreams within an idealistic setting. Yes, measureable goals hold the benefit of being tangibly attainable. While the idealistic latter is much more difficult to physically capture, you are so much more likely to find yourself smiling a whole lot more along the way. Self-fulfillment is an ideal in its own right, and while there are no empirical measures to determine idealistic successes, you'll find that pursuing ideals will give you greater happiness and fulfillment than working toward simple, measurable goals.

Rockstars should have a healthy dose of idealism and optimism about their goal setting. Note that when I refer to goal setting, I don't mean "creating a to-do list of tasks that you need to complete," but instead am referring to the really big stuff that you want to achieve in your life. Perhaps your life goals are to finally quit your corporate job, to establish your own business or to double your annual profits. Your life goals will be specific and unique to you and your personal Rockstardom. Don't worry about the nitty-gritty; instead just allow yourself to dream and be a visionary when setting your life goals.

At the goal setting stage of any project, you should not be fussed about making sure that everything is objective and realistic. So early on, these things don't matter as much. The only limitations that truly exist on any project or new idea are are those that you concoct and unintentionally impose yourself. With enough creativity and energy, you can find a solution for any stumbling block that may impede your achieving a specific goal.

Be as idealistic and optimistic as possible when setting your goals, because when you're shooting to be among the stars and fail at that, you will still have achieved much more than the underachiever that didn't dream to shoot half as high.

It's In Your Hands

Irrespective of any other principle, idea or suggestion in Rockstar Business, you need to understand and accept that the responsibility and accountability with all things Rockstar-related lie squarely on your shoulders - no one else can help you carry that load. Striving to attain dreams, goals, and self-fulfillment is more than strenuous, so if you ultimately come up short, few observers will even bat an eye-lid in surprise (with the contrary being true if you become a rip-roaring success).

In this context, though, you will also find immense empowerment in that you only need to answer to yourself in order to achieve the goals that you have set. Relying upon no one but yourself means that your success will be more personally significant and less superficial than if you relied upon others to achieve your goals.

See, I believe that to a large extent success is in our hands alone, and as Rockstars, we will do everything in our power to achieve that success. The proviso to that is obviously that we cannot control everything within our environments and sometimes when good opportunities don't come knocking, it is simply impossible to create them ourselves.

Whilst the journey may seem pretty lonely when things aren't going as well, the reward is always just on the other side of a potentially unlocked door. Without sounding too much like one of those motivational speakers, I truly believe that Rockstars create their own luck to an extent and because of that, we hold control of our own destinies.

If you can live up to your own high standards, the rest will fall into place. Ultimately, your success is in your own hands and your hands alone.

3 | *Decisions & Values*

Acting the part

Rogue-starness

Defying the black-and-White

Be Impulsive

Don't get caught in the details

Your Risk Boundaries

Make Mistakes

Being Trustworthy

Business isn't just always Business

Transparent Success

It's never about the money

Acting the Part

Now that we are aware of what being a Rockstar is like and, more importantly, that the Rockstar concept must be molded to your own character and personality, we move onto learning about the decisions and values that will sprout forth naturally from the Rockstar-within.

As you become accustomed to feeling like the Rockstar that you are, you need to start thinking like a Rockstar, move your values into alignment with being a Rockstar and finally, to base your decisions on the new concept of Rockstardom. Basically, I'm suggesting that you adopt an "all-inclusive" approach to breathing and living like a Rockstar, since a half-hearted approach just isn't gonna cut it here.

Every single time you think and act like a Rockstar it becomes a more natural process. As a result, what at first requires some concentrated effort gradually becomes habit or second nature. By initially "forcing" yourself to act the part of a Rockstar, you are training yourself to be a better Rockstar, naturally and effortlessly.

In this section, we will explore the decisions and values that can be attributed to Rockstars. In the end, being a Rockstar is not about how much you feel like a Rockstar within yourself - you will ultimately need to prove your Rockstarness (or, otherwise, show your lack thereof) to the outside world. It can only be measured by your actions.

Rogue-starness

Rockstar success is about taking the advice you can use and leaving the rest behind.

Rockstars are rogues in their approach to business. They constantly challenge the viewpoints of others and even their own viewpoints regarding business.

As a Rockstar, it's expected that your ideas and decisions will be different—ideas and decisions that stand out from the norm give you the opportunity to create and achieve the exceptional. You'll make your own mistakes, learn your own lessons and experience your own adventures.

Be an authentic Rockstar and sculpt the rules, ideas and snippets of this book to fit in with your own unique plans.

Defying the Black-and-White

If there's one thing that I've learned about myself, it's that irrespective of how "right" something may feel in our black and white world, I simply can't commit to it if my heart's not committed. This literally means that I would pass up on an easy buck if it just doesn't sit right with me.

Does this mean that Rockstars are irrational and picky?
Definitely not.

However, it does mean that Rockstars recognize that the main reason they do what they do is the fact that their hearts are entrenched in their pursuits. The great thing about that is that our hearts are what set ourselves apart from the next person; ultimately, our hearts play a major role in whether we can live Rockstar lives.

The easiest way to be average is to start following average advice and average rules passed on by average people doing average things in an average job. Get the point? Most of the rules and restrictions we impose on our lives were created by other people: our equals, not any kind of superior human being. So why would you want to do whatever you're told makes sense in the average world, when it contradicts your heart and gut feelings?

Rockstars make decisions that are the best for them personally and for the people around them. The only way to make those kinds of decisions is to stick to what we Rockstars know best: our hearts. Ditch the complicated and contradictory "facts" of the black and white world in favour of the very heart that makes you a Rockstar in the first place.

Be Impulsive

As a Rockstar you'll encounter situations where the best choice will be an impulsive one.

Situations will frequently arise where you will need to make a decision without any time to do traditional planning or analysis. At these times and in these situations, you cannot hit the pause button - Rockstars live, work and play in real-time.

A given situation's window of opportunity is finite and, to stand the chance of exploiting and benefiting from that opportune situation, an impulsive decision will likely be required. In other words, you have to Gut-It-Out: back yourself and trust what your past experiences have taught you.

It is not as risky as it sounds.

The reality is that every decision has an element of risk attached to it. We tend to label that risk as "calculated" because it's less fear inducing. By it's very definition, however, not every single element of risk can be calculated and that's what ultimately makes it a risk. With the nature of risk being what it is, even the most planned and informed of decisions don't always result in success. In many cases, the opportunity can be missed all together.

Don't Get Caught in the Details

More information does not (always) result in a more accurate decision.

Don't get caught up in a details of a decision. When Rockstars try to consider every single possible factor before making a decision, they end up being indecisive rather than sure.

The amount of information should be weighed against the speed at which the decision must be made. Rockstars work in real-time. As a Rockstar, you must remember that (on occasion) you will need to trust your instinct and judgment without having all the information on hand.

Research and fact-finding have their place, and obviously you shouldn't forgo them entirely before reaching a decision. Just bear in mind that not every decision needs to have every potential detail inspected and dissected. Excess details are for the analysts, statisticians and academic researchers to concern themselves with - not us Rockstars.

Where is the Rockstar balance - the middle ground between information and impulse? The balance is found at the point where you, the Rockstar, feel most comfortable making a decision rather than waiting too long for the moment where you have all the necessary information at hand.

Your Risk Boundaries

Some of us are never going to skydive; others will do it every weekend.

Every person has a different risk threshold. It's important to remember that risk isn't a one-size-fits-all item. As a Rockstar, you will need to find your most "comfortably uncomfortable" risk threshold. The only way to do this is by gaining experience.

When you succeed, you learn, and when you fail, you really learn. Both success and failure are both vital tools - each will help you establish your risk boundaries.

Make Mistakes

Being perfect is overrated.

Everyone makes mistakes; it's how we learn. Mistakes are an unavoidable fact of both life and business, and they are one of a Rockstar's greatest assets. They help us get to know ourselves intimately - the good, the bad and the ugly all rear their heads when we make a mistake. This is empowering because it allows us to identify our strengths and weaknesses.

The power is not in being perfect; it's in being human. No one relates to perfection, but everyone relates to being human. By embracing who you are (both the good and the bad), you can interact with anyone, person to person, irrespective of their fame or fortune.

Start viewing your mistakes as beneficial - not bad, detrimental occurrences.

Being Trustworthy

Whilst Rockstar Business suggests that it is perfectly fine to make mistakes every now and again, you need to understand that your mistakes might naturally cause a negative consequence for someone else.

That probably doesn't make much sense, right? I'm saying that it's okay to make mistakes, but the result thereof may hurt someone else - that's obviously not okay. The key here is to be trustworthy in your communication and interactions relating to those mistakes.

Consider this business situation: If you can admit that you have made mistakes and that you are doing X, Y and Z to rectify them, the people who could potentially get hurt (customers, coworkers, etc.) are more likely to give you the benefit of the doubt, since everyone makes mistakes. I think the reason that people tend to spark a "flame war" (that's Internet slang for a heated argument of slander or personal attacks) after someone's mistake or failure is because they have jumped to conclusions (based on their perceptions) concerning the intent of the person who made those mistakes. If you can take those people along on the journey through your thought processes relating to the mistakes, they should be less inclined to start that flame war from the start.

Being trustworthy is about being open, accessible and honest; allowing other people to get close enough to you to get to know the Rockstar-within. This way, you won't be judged purely based on your actions, as those can easily lead to misconceptions. Instead, the people "judging" you will have the context of what kind of person they believe you to be.

Trust can be a difficult achievement, which means that from the get-go you will need to be sensitive about how to go about it properly. But if you're being open, accessible and honest, those things will matter the most as you strive to forge trust with others. Mistakes are bound to happen, but missteps that convey you as dishonest or misleading will create severe collateral damage that will not be as easy to repair.

Business isn't always just Business

After another alienating (and ruthless) blog post, Bob realised: all the gawker traffic wasn't going to make up for the fact that no one trusted him. *If only they'd understand that it wasn't personal; that it was "just business."*

That mythical line that separates business from the personal - as epitomized in the famous Godfather series - is much harder to discern in real life. The famous mafia movies that coined the mantra, "It's not personal, it's business," has no place in the Rockstar Business Model. In reality, business is always personal to someone.

The "It's not personal, it's business" quote has become the businessperson's modern mantra. It has become the way that making decisions that aren't in line with a person's values and morals, somehow OK.

For a Rockstar, business and personal are the same thing. Values, morals and beliefs are important and shouldn't be quickly comprised. Instead of smothering a bad, caveman-like decision with the "It's not personal, it's business" story, we - as Rockstars - need to find a less compromising way to reach the desired outcome.

Embracing Transparency

The Internet - especially with the recent advent of social media - has closed the gap between companies and their customers and stakeholders more than any other business phenomenon in the last couple of years. Many companies have embraced a new level of transparency about their decisions, methods and ultimately, their success.

Rockstar companies and entrepreneurs are no different when it comes to being open and transparent about their success. This is not to say that Rockstars should share trade secrets or competitive advantages that have been built up with years of hard work; instead, being transparent is about embracing a newfound openness and anti-bureaucratic, anti-corporate approach to doing business.

I believe, irrespective of any religious or spiritual convictions, that every business and entrepreneur should feel "blessed" with their success: just as easy as they helped to create it, the people who help fuel one's success can also take it away. Utilizing transparency is all about being ethical and making sound business decisions. When certain business decisions don't work out, that means a Rockstar owns up to those mistakes instead of sweeping them under a rug.

Being Transparent for the Right Reasons

On so many occasions in the past, I've been tempted to be totally transparent and publish the financial results of some of my private business ventures. Whilst that would not have been "wrong" per se (listed companies are obligated to do just this), I would have been doing it for improper reasons: to vindicate my entrepreneurial journeys and to prove wrong all the criticism that I've received.

It's important not to be transparent when you're actually simply reacting to a negative situation, as such behavior that is bound to be viewed as an inappropriate reaction by outside observers. Being transparent is about being proactive about the way you approach your business and the decisions involved with your approach—not about being reactive, vindictive and petty.

Never do the right thing for the wrong reasons; for a Rockstar, that's simply a waste of time.

It's never just about the Money

Rockstars love money for the luxuries it affords them, but their business is never just about the money.

Focusing only on making money will distort creative, unique ideas and thought processes. The very advantages that set us as Rockstars apart from our competitors are smothered when we lose sight of the big picture and become obsessed with making money. Money is a superficial motivator - one that never works in the long term.

Everyone needs some form of long term motivation. Rockstars should look at replacing money with challenges as a primary motivator. One such business-related challenge will ultimately be making money. The difference between a Rockstar and ordinary entrepreneur is that the Rockstar's primary focus has been shifted: the foremost intention becomes less about the money itself and more about succeeding in the challenge of making money.

In this way, a Rockstar makes money become what it should always be: *a reward, not a strategy.*

Decisions should never be just about the money

Rockstars start working the street corner when they make decisions based solely on money.

When Rockstars make business decisions, they should never be based solely on money.

To make great choices you need to consider more than just the money, because money is not the only influencing factor in

41

business. Money is important, of course, but it doesn't exist in a vacuum. With any business decision, there are other vital elements - various keys to success - that are easy to gloss over when money becomes the sole focus.

Business decisions made by a Rockstar should be about the all-encompassing value of the decision, which includes but is not limited to money and profits.

4 | *Spend time outside your own hype*

The Challenge
Rockstar Inspiration
Inspirational Interactions
Online is over-rated
Roots and Hobbies

The Challenge

As you spend time on this journey to Rockstardom—and especially if relative success is involved—you'll find that it becomes more and more difficult to move outside of your own hype and the environment that cultivates that. Whilst hype isn't necessarily a negative thing (to the contrary, its benefits will be explored in the next section), it becomes increasingly important to take your mind outside of that space for continuous inspiration, clarity and vision.

Hype and physical environments are like comfort zones: the more you interact within those spaces, the more you almost limit your mind to only exploring (and getting better at that) the things that you already know.

For example, if you are a web designer, you spend your time in front of the computer screen, designing websites, right? In that case, you will definitely be enhancing your web design skills. However, the drawback is that you are limiting your influences and potential inspiration because you are not exploring beyond the realms of your own design. Similarly, if you only interact with the same group of people on a weekly basis you are only going to get the same feedback and your thoughts will be kept within that box.

The idea is to create an escape from that world and allow yourself to be free to explore other ideas and methods inspiration that will help you stay visionary, unique and of course, a Rockstar.

Allow yourself to be inspired

A Rockstar is never too busy to be inspired.

Inspiration results in great ideas and success in life is based on the realisation of great ideas. Inspiration is an integral part of a Rockstar's make-up. Without inspiration, you, as a Rockstar, are setting yourself up to fail in an unspectacular fashion from the start.

As Rockstars, we need to be able to see beyond the stress and feelings associated with being overworked. We need to move past the vision-clouding comfort zone to a place where we allow inspiration to appear in our lives.

This requires that we undergo a significant mindset shift. To achieve this, Rockstars need to:

Mute the extras

Shut out all the "extras." Inspiration doesn't play nice. It doesn't work when you're stressed, overworked or short of time. Remember, you need inspiration. Take the time to just stop, mute the extras, and the inspiration will find you.

Be in awe

Teach yourself how to Sit-Back-In-Awe. The surrounding world is packed full of inspiration. If you can just get over yourself for long enough, you'll see it. Inspiration is unexpected, unplanned and often completely random.
Just look a little closer, it's right there!

Inspirational Interactions

The best way to grow ideas to their optimised point is to challenge them.

Rockstars enjoy having their ideas challenged because they know that challenging ideas propels their evolution.

When someone challenges our ideas and viewpoints and those challenges hold constructive substance and value, we are afforded the opportunity to revise and improve our original ideas or opinions. Rockstars call these types of constructive challenges "inspirational interactions."

People are traditionally the best source of inspirational interactions. Individuals' differing views, beliefs and opinions mean that wherever you go, as a Rockstar, you're bound to find someone to challenge you.

The goal - what we as Rockstars strive to do - is to be open to these interactions; to put our ego and arrogance aside and hear what the other party is saying. We do so because questions and debate surrounding an idea can strengthen it, help us pinpoint its issues or potential issues, and spark off an even more powerful idea.

Get Out More

The biggest challenge in coming across these inspirational interactions is to actually get yourself out of the office, away from the desk and to free yourself from your surroundings a little. Just as you can have inspirational interactions within those spaces, it's likely that you're so accustomed to routine interactions around the office by now that you've been blunted from seeing their real potential. By actually putting yourself in other environments and interacting with different people, you're much more likely to gain that inspiration.

Going out can mean hooking up with some like-minded business friends or just running out for a cup of coffee, even if you need to take your laptop along. Just a small change in scenery or a shakeup in your routine should get some other ideas working in your mind.

The bottom line seems to be that inspiration is not always in the things we look at every day, because we're often just "too close" to those things to view them holistically and objectively. Rockstars understand that a little break within their routines should be more than enough kindling to create a few sparks of inspiration.

Online is Overrated

If you know my story, you know that up until this point my business ventures (the successful one's at least) have been restricted to "the interwebs." This means that although I have had the "privilege" of spending most of my day behind a computer screen and with immense ease can access the online world, I actually need to force myself to get offline.

I'm not saying that I think primarily being a web entrepreneur is a bad situation, but every good situation has its own downside. The important aspect for me has been realizing the "other side" of that same coin. Now, I can see online business for what it is: just another industry.

It is my perception that more and more people are flocking to the Internet and online entrepreneurship because they believe that there's easy money to be made. The reality is that it is just as difficult or as easy to make online as it is in any other industry. If your Rockstar Business involves you being keen to follow those sheep, then at least consider it objectively before you jump online, because the supposed "awesomeness" thereof is most definitely overrated.

I may add that the Internet has obviously changed the way that most of our modern businesses operate. Irrespective of whether your business is focused on building or harnessing online communities, or whether you just use the Internet as another tool in your business, you need to find ways to go offline (and, "online" here also means being confined to your office; you don't need to be surfing the web all day for this to be applicable).

Having a nice, comfortable desk and chair with everything you need (WiFi, coffee, X-Box, etc.) around you is definitely awesome but overrated in the sense that it becomes redundant when you don't venture outside of that space often enough. Sometimes you just need to "switch off," go offline, and go back to the old school ways of living, where things like your personal hobbies, meeting new people and enjoying the company of friends were more important.

Roots & Hobbies

Being a Rockstar is secondary to the rest of one's life.

Everyone has pre-Rockstar roots and hobbies that will contribute to one's journey toward exploring and cultivating a Rockstar persona. Whilst one becomes so busy in pursuing these Rockstar ideals, it is so easy to forget where we came from and how our hobbies and passions have helped to shape the men and women that we have become today.

Part of your challenge as a Rockstar is to fill your time with enough of your "roots" so that you will never forget who you are as a person. It's furthermore important to remember your roots because reminiscing about where you once were and where you are now gives you a much more holistic view of your life. Reminiscing about one's life in such a way also takes you away from the comfort zones and boundaries that we erect around ourselves, thus giving much more context to your daily decisions and actions.

The best way to return to these "roots" is by way of the hobbies that you are most passionate about. The idea here is not necessarily to sit and contemplate one's life, but instead, you should strive to "lose yourself" within some meaningless enjoyment and indulgence of those hobbies. The benefit is that you will provide yourself with a much needed break from the goals you always seem to be chasing - taking a break and losing yourself in your hobbies will help you feel mentally refreshed and inspired to keep pursuing your goals and dreams.

There's also another case for why your roots and hobbies remain important, regardless of what you are pursuing in the Rockstar

Business areas of your life. Your soul, personality and identity are naturally entrenched in the spaces of your roots and hobbies, and I'd bet that because of all the passion that is generated there you are more than likely to find a few great ideas by sifting through the "information" available to you about yourself when you indulge in them.

Your hobbies will help bring you balance and serve as an escape from an unbalanced, "business-only" pursuit. Your roots will keep you grounded (amongst your great Rockstar successes) without weighing you down.

5 *Branding*

You are the Brand
Personal vs Business Branding
Be Yourself
Personal Responsiveness
Don't stereotype yourself
Make time for Others
Nobody is Bigger than You
Whorestar
Being the Expert
Branding in Practice

You are the brand

The branding portion of being a Rockstar is either going to be the easiest or most difficult part to explain in the whole book, simply because most people seem to ignore the benefits of viewing yourself - a unique individual - as a marketable brand. So, we're going to need a little bit of a mind shift here…

Brands exist all around us and if we were to be quizzed to name a few popular brands, I'm sure that your "Top Ten" would consist of only the most popular products or product-related companies. The reality, however, is that there are many famous people (such as celebrities and "A-Listers") in the world that, whilst you may not consider them as brands, have such great recognition and advertising power as household names that it places them in the same bracket as the leading brands and companies across the globe.

Looking at an ordinary definition of the word "brand," you would find that a brand is a name or image generally associated with a product, service or business. Elaborating on that very basic concept, you would also discover that a "brand image" is a psychological construct of various people's opinions of and connotations about a particular brand. Considering this, we could probably safely include people as brands, along with products and companies, because it is totally possible to associate a name, an image and a few opinions and connotations with a unique individual.

Those are just the academics.

The fact is, just as you may strive to build brands within your companies, you also have one very important brand that you need to nurture and market: yourself. We will get into a bit of "how-to" for personal branding now. It's important to first understand that proper branding is integral to the makeup and success of a Rockstar, since our whole aim is to connect with real people based on who we truly are, what we do and how we go about doing it. In my mind, your average person, consumer or follower will find it easier to connect and interact with another person over to a "dead" brand. To an extent, your personal branding should be far superior to any of the inanimate brands that you create through your business activities.

You are your own brand and you already have all of the ingredients (your unique character, personality, decisions and values) to build and nurture that brand. The next section will explore a few ways in which you can establish that Rockstar brand and start to make it work for you.

Personal vs Business Branding

There's a clear difference between personal and business branding. While the same marketing rules apply to both, these two branding areas should be treated as separate, individual brands.

Your personal brand should exist independent from your various business brands, because:

#1 - You are a human being and your brand should reflect that. Your personal branding thus needs to take different considerations into account because you have different goals compared to that of a business brand.

#2 - By creating an independent personal brand, you are firstly diversifying your risk and business interests since you are building an audience in your personal capacity. This means that in the future, you will be able to leverage your personal audience and "push" new business ideas and ventures at them because they follow and trust you - not only your previous business brands.

Whilst this separation and independence makes sense, it's important to consider that any successes or failures you will have with your business brands has the appropriate influence on your personal brand (and vice versa). Thus, your personal brand is never completely isolated from your business brands.

This is, however, a great situation since you can build two separate brands - business and personal - with slightly different audiences at the same time, and while doing the same things. For example, if you launch a new marketing campaign and your business brand flourishes as a result, you will get a lot of personal kudos (if people are aware that you and your personal brand are behind those great ideas and implementation thereof) for those business successes.

Be Yourself

Even in his flawless disguise, every Twitterer at the party knew that he wasn't one of them; his inability to state what he was doing - in 140 characters or less - was a dead giveaway.

It can be tempting, especially when you're just starting out, to pretend to be someone or something that you're not.

Often and when there's something business related to be gained, we doubt ourselves and our ability. We replace self-belief with the belief that becoming someone or something - other than who we are - will (in given circumstances) result in more business. But in reality, attempting to become someone that you are not won't result in more business and it certainly won't result in the right type of business.

Your brand is as much about who you are as it is about who you're not. Be yourself and leverage that brand to its fullest potential.

It is so important when you focus on personal branding that you don't betray who you are and what you stand for, as your branding would be superficial and flimsy without these values (which serve as a kind of backbone). This is especially significant when you consider how many self-proclaimed "successful" people we meet every day, and as a result, how we've developed the inherit ability to spot a potential fake.

Your "truth" in your personal branding is relative to your honesty, transparency and willingness to admit that you're not as perfect as your branding could falsely suggest. So whilst you're not going to trumpet your imperfections, you can still just be normal and just be yourself.

Personal Responsibility

Whether Rockstars are at work or at play, they are still the same people.

As Rockstars, we're in touch with who we are; our work is merely an extension of our already-existent life. To achieve lasting success, the choices that we make (from a work point of view) must be in alignment with our personal goals, dreams, ideals, and needs.

Before we became Rockstars, many of us as entrepreneurs and businesspeople wrongly expected ourselves to invest absolutely everything in our businesses. This came at the expense of our personal goals, dreams, ideals and needs. Rockstars value themselves and their personal happiness as a priority - in fact, it's a major cornerstone and a unique ingredient of their success.

A Rockstar needs to constantly evaluate the projects he or she is involved in. Anything that doesn't align with a Rockstar's goals, dreams, ideals and needs should be improved upon or removed completely. The more you (as a Rockstar) work on this personal and professional alignment, the more efficient you'll become.

If you find something isn't working for you, whether it's a project or a something relating to your own behavior, take the initiative and make the change.

You are a Rockstar and you have the freedom to act instinctively, altering anything you believe is holding you back.

Don't Stereotype Yourself

Stereotypes are so twentieth century.

People like stereotypes. Labels put us at ease because it means we belong and we know others belong too. The more that we share with a group's values and principles, the more akin to them we feel.

We learn early that it is easier to be a stereotype than it is to be unique. Being "different" is frowned upon and incites castigations, so from an early age people limit their outlook and opportunities in order to "belong" to the norm. Individuals are taught to measure their ideas, dreams and successes against expected criteria. Anything that doesn't match up to the status quo ought to be ignored or rejected. Original thinking is discarded. Why do we let this happen to ourselves?

Belonging to a group or conforming to a stereotype is incredibly tempting to many people because it makes them feel safe. They have a predictable behaviour pattern against which they can measure themselves as equals. Rockstars reject this. "Belonging" is not what drives a Rockstar.

Rockstars define their own vision and are pushed by their own creativity - a community stereotype concept will never suffice. A Rockstar's thinking is not restricted by the limitations of stereotypical behaviours and Rockstars measure the success of their strategies by their own unique criteria.

Leave the labels and stereotypes to those that need them; Rockstars don't fit in boxes.

Make Time for Others

One of my biggest gripes in life is the fact that some people are just so darn inaccessible. By this I mean that it doesn't matter how many e-mails you send them; you just don't ever get a response (because they're the supposed Rockstar and you're only the peasant).

The problem with that is that one's ignorance and arrogance will unfortunately not take you very far anymore...
I understand that successful people are generally successful because they're also busy and working away on some new fascinating project. However, that doesn't mean that they shouldn't connect with the people that reach out to them. It's probably similar to being a big Hollywood celebrity; those celebs are harassed on a daily basis for autographs, photographs, etc., but the best of them handle it all with a smile, irrespective of how fed-up they might be.

Why do they do it? Because that's how you treat your fans.

Fans deserve your respect and time, just as much as you enjoy yours. A true Rockstar thus creates time within his or her schedule to connect with fans on a regular basis. Within every of those interactions, there's a further opportunity to market yourself to those fans and create an even better reputation for yourself.

People definitively dislike arrogance and you would be creating a true test of your fans' loyalties should they be continuously ignored.

The ironic thing is that even a simple, one-line note via e-mail is sometimes enough of a response to these fans. Sometimes you will be required to invest a little more time to respond accordingly, but generally fans just want to know that even though you're busy, they can still reach you (irrespective of how unimportant they feel in comparison).

When you respond to the people who reach out to you, these fans will continue to breed loyalty for your Rockstar brand - it's almost dead certain that they'll continue to wax lyrical about you, not because you are the Messiah, but because you are a genuine and humble person.

Nobody is Bigger than You

They may have more Twitter followers, but that's a different story for a different day.

When you're a fledgling Rockstar, it's tempting to be intimidated by established and successful entrepreneurs. Society adds these people to the untouchable and unapproachable "Hall of Fame" and we mark them up as "off-limits."

When we see the most successful and respected of entrepreneurs at a business or social event, we don't dare approach them for fear of rejection. They become the ridiculously good-looking girl at the party, the one everyone looks at but no one has the guts to talk to.

The truth is that, as every beginner Rockstar comes to realise, the famed "hot girl" entrepreneurs are just people like us, who happen to be successful. Some of them will be friendly and approachable. Others won't be.

Novice Rockstars who get over their fears will discover - and be pleasantly surprised by - just how generous many great business-people are with their time and willingness to offer advice from their experiences.

Whorestar

"Whore" is a very derogatory word in today's societies, but instead the "street-walker" should be lauded for their self-marketing and self-promotional efforts. As a Rockstar, you can definitely learn a little from that.

Of course, I'm being tongue-in-cheek. I'm not suggesting that you actually become an active member of the sex industry, but there's no reason why you shouldn't market yourself to the extent that people would want to label you as a "whore." What does that actually mean though?

People can only remember and follow you if they actually know about you. Why wait for other people to spread the word virally, when you can do some the talking yourself? There's absolutely nothing wrong with a Rockstar doing their own talking and marketing - so long as your marketing efforts are truthful and you're being yourself, of course. I believe in taking some control over what is said about you. Plus, sitting back and waiting for things to happen virally is a little too passive for my inner Rockstar.

Ultimately, if others want to play "pin the label" on you, then let them waste their time. You'll be too busy telling other people how to be a (Whore)Rockstar.

Experts

Compared to my "Whorestar" marketing ideas in the previous chapter, my Rockstar strategies regarding expertise and marketing will be considerably less controversial: As a Rockstar, you must market yourself as an expert within your niche, even if you may not have all of the knowledge and experience generally required to be understood as an expert.

Before we get into how you can become an expert, we need to look at how our societies identify their experts. Generally speaking, the experts among us are either academic giants with their Ph.D.'s and MBA's or are seasoned, well-travelled and obscenely rich founders and CEOs of big companies. There is also another field of supposed experts and they come in the form of best-selling authors. I mean, who is going to argue with someone who has sold millions of books on his topic of interest?

The difficult part here is convincing Average-Joe-Public that you are indeed an expert and thus worthy of their attention. This is further complicated by the rules that we have inherited in our societies and we thus have to find a fine balance between playing by those rules and defying them in a Rockstar-like manner.
Becoming the Expert

Becoming a self-marketed "expert" means that you need to show people that you have a great understanding of your niche and that you know how to profit (whether financially or otherwise) from that knowledge and experience. Your strategy is thus two-fold:

#1 - You need to tell people about your knowledge and experiences by sharing those with them on a blog, by self-publishing a book (it can be a downloadable e-book), and speaking at conferences. All of those mediums (especially publishing a book and speaking at conferences) will go a long way to establish an aura of expertise around your brand. People love insight into the way that successful people think and how they go about engineering that success. Provide value for them by sharing your experiences and knowledge, and you're already closer to being an expert in their opinion.

#2 - The first step can only be successful if you have had some related and relative success in terms of the experiences and knowledge that you are sharing. It doesn't matter how well you can communicate these facts in theory; people will only assign you credibility if you can prove to them that what you are saying actually works (i.e. you need to be practicing what you are preaching).

There is only value and viability if you are marketing genuine substance, because you are not going to become an expert based on superficial facts. Your audience will also be quick to realize any superficial information and would lead to them to quickly ignore your future attempts at marketing your expertise.
Tipping Point: Recommendations

The tipping point for your expert branding will come in the viral form of word of mouth: the more other people start talking about you and what you're doing, the more credible your messages become.

Large parts of our societies are followers and they accept "facts" based on popular opinion. So if you can get a bunch of people honestly and objectively (i.e. this needs to be truthful and there's no way to "buy" these opinions) say loads of positive stuff about you, then these followers are bound to believe the hype and "adopt" the idea that you must indeed be an expert. Afterwards, the viral pyramid comes into play and if your marketing messages have enough legs, you should find it snowballing as your expert brand just continues to grow.

The tipping point effect is made even more significant when you get some kind words from influential people, as this just adds immense and exponential significance to that snowball effect. Make sure that your branding and marketing appeals to influential people and then ensure that they are actually exposed to those messages in their normal day-to-day activities. Rockstars realize that influential people are probably not going to go out of their way to look for you.

Branding in Practice

This is somewhat of a checklist to make sure that you are optimizing your personal branding activities:

#1 - If you're online, you need to make sure that you have registered your personal domain (or a derivative thereof), along with that username on the social networks that you are going to frequent (and which should contribute to business goals). For example, if you want to be known as "Adii" online, then it would be great to have the http://adii.com or http://adii.me domain, as well as http://twitter.com/adii on Twitter and a few other social networks.

#2 - Regardless of whether or not you are a good writer or communicator, you do need a blog of some sort. This can take the form of a traditional blog where you write a lot, or a Tumblog (Tumblr.com) where you simply share some ideas and thoughts whenever you feel the urge. Blogging serves as a way of making you more accessible to your followers. They will appreciate a more in-depth look at your Rockstar persona. If writing and content creation is not really for you, then at minimum you need an aggregated profile that links out to all of your projects, the social networks you frequent and includes biographical information about yourself.

#3 - Attend conferences in your niches, and, even better, try presenting at one of those. Networking in person still beats any other form of interaction and it is much easier to market yourself in person than it is though more static mediums, such as on the Internet.

#4 - Become friendly with other Rockstars in your own and related niches and industries. It's great to have friends and it's always inspirational to interact with them. On top of that, you may just get a recommendation or two from them, which may open doors that would not have been unlocked otherwise. Your relationships with these well-followed Rockstars will also endear you to their audiences and add further credibility to your own reputation.

#5 - Make it easy for others to contact you and if they e-mail you, please do respond. Every single interaction with another person is a marketing exercise and you have an opportunity to create a fan for life by just adding value and responding accordingly to a simple e-mail.

#6 - Ensure that your personal brand is obviously linked to your business brands, so that their respective successes and growth can feed the other.

#7 - Your visual identity is just as important as your words, actions and reputation. So get a few proper photos taken of yourself and reuse them whenever and wherever you can. Company brands have the edge here, because they have visual logos that they use to appeal to their audience. You need to leverage your own visual identity to achieve a similar effect. Of course, you don't have to be a model - people just want to see what you look like because they can then better relate to you and connect on a more human and personal level.

#8 - Personal branding isn't easy, especially if you've never done it before. The key is to simply decide on a strategy and then keep bashing away at your goals and aims. Your audience will appreciate your consistency and you are bound to start building a credible reputation and following if you can just outlast your "competition" (i.e. the competing brands that also vie for the attention of your prospective audience).

6 | *The Business*

6.1 The Team
6.2 The Ideas
6.3 Running the Business Model

6.1 | *The Team*

Basics with regards to human capital within a business.

Business is about People
Surrounding yourself with great people
Picking your team
Culture
Getting help from the start
Sharing wealth and incentives
Taking a Personal Interest
Never limit Anyone or Anything
Creativity at all costs

Business is about People

The most vital resource in any business is human capital.

In the aggressive business environments that Rockstars tend to frequent, phenomenal employees separate the great organisations from the good.

The combination of exceptional employees and their various (and, in some cases, polar) opinions and experiences result in the most unique ideas, approaches or solutions, all of which unquestionably benefit the business.

These employees and their ideas don't just appear; they're a direct product of their work environment.

In order to attract - and retain - the best human capital, Rockstars need to create and maintain the type of environment that appeals to these employees and helps them flourish. Establishing this environment is about knowing your employees and using your knowledge about them to add the right type of value to their work.

Rockstars know their employees. They attract and retain the best human capital by utilising this knowledge to create and maintain business environments that add real value to their workforce.

At radiiate, I've always tried to build the type of company that would appeal to the team and create a refreshing and passionate environment in which team members can get their jobs done. That environment has included things like free lunches, xBox and Nintendo Wii breaks and 4-day workweeks have been part of the company culture from the very beginning. I institute these elements in our work culture to place emphasis on the fact that our business is not just about clients, deadlines and financial statements, but also about the people that I need to get the jobs done.

Surrounding Yourself with Great People

Whilst you are in the process of deciding the makeup of the team that will help you achieve your business goals, it is vital to always remember the how your team has helped your success: you cannot once entertain any arrogance toward or ignorance of your team. When things are going well, we tend to believe that we can conquer the world, but the value of having an incredible team to support you should never be underrated. In the end, any combination of arrogance and ignorance will only skew your business decisions.

It would be easy to use clichés such as "a team is only as strong as its weakest link," and "a team is stronger than the individuals on that team," but the reality is that the better the people you surround yourself with, the greater your chance of dealing with the challenges of the business environment in a successful way.

The quality of your team members will directly influence your business output on a daily basis. They will also influence your own mindset and actions significantly. It's almost a case of only being able to lead a team to the measure of success that they allow; if your team members are happy with being average then your ability to lead them will be superb, but the output of your business will be average, too.

In a Rockstar Business, it's really important to surround yourself with the best people for your job (remember that your requirements are unique) and whilst they might not be Rockstars yet, you should identify the potential that your team members have, realizing that they could be proper Rockstars in the future.

I have twice experienced the opposite of what I preach above, when I added some interns to our team that weren't such "great" people. Not only did they not gel with the other team members, but also their personalities didn't fit in with the company culture that we had created internally. Suffice to say that they lasted two weeks and three months respectively before they moved on... In stark contrast, the rest of the radiiate team has been around for ages and the greatness that they bring just continues to grow and evolve.

Picking your Team

When it comes to compiling your team, you shouldn't look to hire already-made Rockstars. At the risk of sounding hypocritical here, I think that the odds are that already-established Rockstars will be too expensive, have too much experience (in other words, they may be inflexible) and they have a chip on their shoulders from their sustained success to this point in time.

Suffice to say, I'm not a big advocate of head-hunting, either.

I believe in unearthing the raw talent and then polishing that into a more Rockstar form. For example, I would rather pick a hard-working, committed and loyal person over the obscenely talented one every single time; talent fades away when it cannot find a proper fit within the team environment. While characteristics like loyalty and dedication are perhaps less spectacular than unbeliev-able talent, team members who exemplify these traits will breed a stronger team culture that nurtures humility whilst always contrib-uting to business value.

Remember: your business is unique. The requirements placed on your team will also be specific to what you need to achieve. A great candidate in general could possibly be your second or third choice if you consider their credentials within the context of your unique needs. Keep this in mind when you are looking at the combination of individuals on your team: their individual contributions aren't that important when considered individually. However, those contributions, when combined with those of the rest of the team, will be extremely valuable.

Finding the balance

When picking your team, remember to find proper balance. Consider your own personal needs and the influences that your team members will have on you. Your first step should be in picking team members that compliment your way of thinking and doing things. Having team members with similar personalities and values to your own will allow for less friction within your interactions, thus making the rest of your business decisions more streamlined.

There is an important balance to find in this, though, considering that you also need team members who can contribute an alternate angle to the conversation - what we referred to earlier as inspirational interactions. Whilst I wouldn't suggest that you hire someone that is the complete opposite of you, a Rockstar doesn't need or want exact clones of oneself. Differences in your opinions and ideas against those of your team should be embraced, as real value is found within that fusion of varying ideas and thought processes.

More than two years since starting radiiate, the first two members of the team are still involved in the company (even though they have moved on to my other business, WooThemes, full-time). When I hired Cobus (a.k.a. FRESH01) and Foxinni, neither of them came with glowing reputations or extensive CV's and portfolios. Instead, I saw their potential when I had met with them and immediately felt that their personalities would be a great fit for the company and the team that I was looking to build.

The best thing about both of these decisions is the fact that I've seen both Cobus and Foxinni develop as designers and developers, as well as individuals. Both of them are much more rounded and experienced in terms of their work today; the benefit of having such amazing people around you is infinite.

I also trust that this approach is serving radiiate very well with our two most recent acquisitions to the team - Cobus E. and Marie - who both fit the same mould that Cobus and Foxinni did when they first joined the team.

Culture

I cannot even begin to express the importance of the culture of your business. Culture is vital, and not only if you have employees: a bad business culture and working environment will also impact your own ability to be Rockstar. By entrenching the right values, principles and philosophies into your daily business environment, you will start cultivating more positive behaviour in return.

Business culture applies to you whether you are a single freelancer or working within a team. However, it becomes even more important when you are the employer or hold a leadership position because the rest of your team takes their cues from the culture that you create. If you're only going to do the minimum amount of work, then those around you won't feel overly inclined to do much more than their job descriptions require, either. By exemplifying a hardworking attitude yourself, you lead by example: your team will notice your work ethic and begin contributing more, themselves.

In Rockstar Business, we've already discussed many of the attributes, characteristics and values that we associate with being a Rockstar. When it comes to business culture, you need to communicate these principles to those around you - both through your actions and your words. You set the tone for how everything happens within your business; the better the example that you set, the better the ultimate result.

The greatest value is not in having one Rockstar in your business (you), but in having multiple Rockstars as they learn the cultural guidelines you have implemented with your own behaviour and begin to operate accordingly. Ten Rockstars are much better than one.

I hate being the boss - this is probably the most significant indication of an unique company culture at radiiate. I have always encouraged the team to set their own culture in terms of how they work and interact with me and other team members.

I prefer an extremely transparent culture in which team members can be empowered rather than limited. This means that team members are even aware of company financials and project sizes because such considerations can help influence their decisions just as much as it does my own as employer and manager. The fact that they have access to this data, I believe, has empowered them to make informed decisions about their work in an otherwise very informal, flexible culture and company structure.

Don't do everything yourself

Rockstars understand that help isn't a swear word.

The "jack-of-all-trades," "D.I.Y." mentality that is so prominent in successful small businesses (and for traditional entrepreneurs) does not work in the world of the Rockstar.

Rockstars shouldn't be using their time for activities that distract them from their core skills. They need to focus on developing and improving the expertise that has set them apart from other people and businesses. Without consistent work, practice and attention, it's very easy for a Rockstar to lose his edge.

That's not to say that a Rockstar can't help someone else out - Rockstars are never above any task. However, Rockstars should often reflect upon and remember where their personal abilities lie, thus spending the majority of their time focusing on developing and practicing their areas of expertise.

The more that Rockstars concentrate and build on their talents, the more likely they are to succeed.

Get help from the start

When a Rockstar is starting out in business, it may not be financially viable or actually possible to hire an entire team that one desires. Nevertheless, Rockstars should look at hiring as soon as they need and can afford to do so.

Getting help is not about hiring for the sake of hiring. Another team member should only be added if it is believed that he or she will make an significant contribution to the business. Rockstars aren't floatation devices; they don't carry dead weight or luxury hires.

A strong business cannot be built without sharing some of the business responsibilities. Allowing others to help and contribute to the business and bottom-line is a part of the Rockstar mindset.

Don't forget to contribute yourself

As a Rockstar, it is vital that you contribute to your business as well. It's not just about contributing from a strategic point of view, but also getting involved in the day-to-day stuff.

Rockstars need understand how their business works so they, and the people they hire, can add real value through their decisions and actions.

Running a business is not admin

It's vital for entrepreneurs to get help from the start and expand their teams as their businesses grow, purely because you must avoid getting caught up only in the nitty-gritty of running your business.

From a Rockstar point-of-view, such a micromanaged corporate approach will kill natural inspiration and decision-making processes within a business by overloading oneself with paper work and formal how-to's. In the end, business owners find themselves handling more admin work and managing chaos than being the leader of the team with an inspirational vision.

Handling administrative tasks definitely does not constitute running a business. This isn't to say that Rockstars look down upon the administrative responsibilities within a business - they are requirements and integral to building a successful company - but that they should never be the sole responsibility of the business owner.

No Rockstar can function without having a proper basis or foundation from which they can operate. Proper administrative structures provide those foundations for operations and allow a Rockstar to focus on what matters the most. Trust in the fact that there are people who are great at handling administrative tasks and that these people can do it in a third of the time that you can.

Clearing up your time to enable you to lead, conceptualize new ideas and just be inspirational isn't only cost-efficient, but it is pretty darn Rockstar at that. Stick to the things that make you a Rockstar - I highly doubt your Rockstardom is rooted in handling mundane administrative stuff.

I probably didn't get help as early as I should have, but about 9 months into the growth of radiiate, I hired Dom to become my business and personal assistant. At that stage, I was forced to spend my time handling a lot of admin-related issues (project quotations, invoicing, sorting out bank accounts, etc.), which became a complete drain on my ability to run the business and contribute to it (designing and developing at that time).

To say that Dom has had a major influence along the way would be a significant understatement. Having her help me with the stuff that kept falling off my radar has meant that I have more free time and more flexibility to manage the team and have a more holistic, strategic approach to the business. My days are now also spent doing the stuff I like and am actually good at (administrative duties have never been one of my Rockstar skills).

Sharing Wealth & Incentives

Earlier we discussed both the significant and insignificant roles of money within a Rockstar Business. The exact same principles are extremely relevant when employees are considered.

Start by considering the culture that you have set: what importance and focus does your culture have on money and earnings? Whilst a great salary package will always entice prospective employees to join your business, it should not be the main attraction. Try to take the focus away from the financials associated with working within your business and instead motivate existing and prospective employees with other incentives, such as a creative work environment and allowing team members to pursue self-fulfillment.

That said, money still makes the world go 'round and it is extremely important that you reward team members accordingly. I'm not from the school of thought whereby it is only the business owners or directors that have an interest in the profitability of the business. I'm instead attracted to a setup where the wealth and continued success of the business can be shared amongst the whole team.

I believe that it is perfectly fair for a business's owners to pocket the most profit, as it is ultimately they who have undertaken the greatest risks involved in setting up the business and underwriting the overheads when they've had no income. The risk and reward should be matched. But when a company is 100% more profitable this year compared to the year previous, part of that additional profitability needs to be distributed to the team that ultimately made that possible.

Distribution of additional profits doesn't need to be in the form a profit-sharing agreement of sorts, and it could also simply take the shape of a basic salary increase; the important consideration is that the financial reward is in line with the contribution (directly or indirectly to the additional profitability) of a team member.

From the perspective of employees, this obviously serves as a huge incentive to work even harder as they now have an interest in the overall well-being of the business. Distribution of additional profits also shows good faith on your side - it should go a long way toward endearing yourself to your team.

I mentioned in the chapter about company culture that I have always been transparent to my team about the financials of the company. This has had two implications for the team: 1) they know exactly how much revenue they need to generate to "carry their own weight" and contribute to general overheads; and 2) they have incentives of receiving profit sharing and future shares if they do great work.

I also have an arrangement with the team on all project ideas that they bring to the table: if it becomes a success and turns into a sustainable business, they become the owner of that part of the business and will receive profit-sharing shares in that project. Simple incentives make the world of difference in this regard.

Taking a personal interest

Business and friendship generally don't mix well, but it is impossible to ignore the positive effect of having a great business relationships with the members of your team. You need to find a balance between building a friendship in the context of the professional environment and a relationship that is suitable to that environment.

Start by really getting to know your team - both as individuals and as a unit - so you can begin to strategize around their strengths and weaknesses. The only way to find these strengths and weaknesses is to take a keen interest in every individual's life: consider one's background, one's existing circumstances, and one's actions within the business. Establishing a "human" understanding of the employee will also help you to recognize any changes in their mental state or body language that could potentially affect their work contributions, thus giving you the opportunity to rectify adverse behaviours before they have far-reaching implications in your business performance.

Beyond the obvious benefits for your business, investing a personal interest in your team members shows that you consider them important as human beings, not only as a profit-earning employees. It may seem small, but such a sign of good faith will go far in establishing a fruitful relationship between employer and employee.

Many of us are friends outside of the office - not best friends, but when we do hang out we always have a great time. I have also taken quite a personal approach with the individuals on the team in terms of getting to know them outside of the business environment, which probably means that in some cases I've become an "older brother" type figure on the team.

Never limit anyone or anything

Being boxed and labeled really brings out the claustrophobia in employees. Who knew?

Traditional organisations are all about limits and controls: specific job descriptions, day-to-day To-Do lists and fixed employee financial packages. Every aspect of the organisation, including its employees, is controlled.

The negative aspect (one of a few) associated with control is its limiting nature. So, why not just throw it out the window? Well, that wouldn't work! An element of control is important. There is always a need for checks and balances in business - safeguards in place that ensure things are working the way that they should. Nevertheless, perhaps the ways in which we, as Rockstars, tender our methods of control is where the change should happen.

As a Rockstar, you'll often find yourself treading the fine line between complete freedom and greatly reduced control. It's not about "limiting" but rather about reaching desired outcomes without prescribing the "how."

Rockstars understand that constructed limitations are based on the constructor's own opinion. Rockstars also have enough humility to admit that they don't always know what's best.

Start challenging your own views and conceptions; trust yourself and those whom you hire to get their jobs done in their own ways.

87

When radiiate came out of a 10-month hibernation at the start of 2010, we set out to build a company that had unlimited possibilities: so we had no pre-defined limitations on what clients we took on, which products we were trying to build or the industries we sought to attack with new solutions. This approach led us down a scattered journey, where we were grasping at different ideas, but none becoming viable. Therefore, it is only recently that this "open canvas" approach started coming to fruition...

Once we got some help in terms of brainstorming ideas and empowering the team to pursue these ideas, the benefits became obvious. At the time of Rockstar Business going to print, awesome client work has started to flow in whilst we continue to work on two amazing internal projects - all of which was generated in this "impossible is nothing" environment (borrowing a slogan from Adidas) within radiiate.

Creativity at all costs

I've found that creative work environments are an absolute necessity within any Rockstar Business; not only is it an absolute blast working in a fun and quirky workplace, but establishing such a mentality contributes to very happy employees and a strong company culture.

The obvious benefit of having employees who are happy and inspired in their workplace is that their state of mind invites a greater boost in their productivity and the value and significance of their contributions. It becomes a quid pro quo situation: when employees feel rewarded and loved, you would be foolish to ignore the positive consequences that stem from their happiness.

If you nurture a creative work environment in the right way, you invite your team of happy employees to get involved in generating business ideas of their own. Consider that your team (yourself included) consists of the only people that know your business inside-out; ideas generated from within could potentially be very viable and profitable. Inviting team members to generate business ideas also takes a lot of weight from your shoulders as the visionary and chief strategist to produce all of the great ideas.

The creative work environment comes down to not limiting your team members in any way. Give them the creative space to explore new solutions and ideas within the framework of also getting their required tasks and jobs done; the value that this Rockstar approach will add to your business will be significant!

In a similar way that I've always tried to create a blank canvas for the team, creativity has always been encouraged. If this means that we need to spend more time out of the office than in it to get over some creative block, that's what needs to happen. Creativity is more important than delivering fast work or meeting deadlines. Quality, not quantity.

6.2 | *The Ideas*
How to choose ideas based on business plans / models.

The Planning Stage
Out of the Box
Be Vigilent
Ignore the competition
Balancing Contingencies
Picking the Right Idea

The Planning Stage

Earlier in Rockstar Business, we discussed the importance of not becoming caught up in the minor details of each decision because the more that information is available to you doesn't necessarily guarantee a more accurate or better decision. Once you have your mind set on exploring a new business, project or idea, not getting caught up in the nitty-gritty aspects becomes extremely important; that obsession will cripple what progress could be made.

Rockstars possess the ability (if they don't naturally, they can develop and nurture it) to take calculated risks and have some impulsiveness to throw themselves headlong into a new idea. But taking risks comes from one's passions and gut-feelings that the idea will work; so if you're not feeling that, then don't even enter the planning stage for the idea, as you're only going to waste your time.

I'm not a big fan of making elaborate forecasts and considering every possible future eventuality for new ideas - to me, that's mostly just speculation. In a similar way, I don't really trust budgets: they are either irrelevant (when based on historic data) or guesswork (when they try to simulate future possibilities). Rockstars are best advised not to waste time on forecasting future events or meticulously budgeting projects - if you become even remotely stuck on those, you will feel your inspiration for your idea drain very quickly.

The trick for the Rockstar when planning is to strike a balance of being impulsive, being willing to take a calculated risk, and making sure that you have your facts straight. If your idea is to reinvent the wheel, then you at least need some facts that your wheel will actually be a viable product and that you will have a good chance to grab some market share from competitive products. If not, then you're being unrealistic: your approach is unbalanced and overly impulsive and risky.

When we evaluate new ideas to determine whether it's worthwhile pursuing them or not, budgets, business models and speculation are secondary to the core of the design: if we feel passionate about the idea and we can see ourselves using it (and enjoying the development thereof), then it's worthwhile pursuing in more depth.

It is only in the second round of evaluating ideas that we start to look at the nitty-gritty of a specific idea and whether it can be viable and profitable, because of course they remain important to a business. Nevertheless, our approach allows the idea to gather momentum (as fueled by our passion) before we become overly conservative in evaluating the "boring" considerations such as revenue models and budgets.

Out of the Box

Finding and identifying new ideas normally isn't a problem for Rockstars: you have become a natural at creating all the right inspirational opportunities for yourself to conceptualize new businesses and projects. Even still, you'll soon realize that not every one of your ideas will be viable or potentially turn into a sustainable and profitable venture. As you go on the journey of exploring each new idea, you will also find that it becomes harder to generate ideas outside of a specific headspace.

Your challenge as a Rockstar is to explore as many avenues, industries and markets as possible in the search of the next great idea. Every Rockstar will have a fondness to a particular niche and that niche will most likely end up being your cash cow going forward. Nevertheless, this doesn't mean that you should limit yourself to only exploring the possibilities within that space.

There is great value in exposing yourself to as many different business models as possible: you could potentially learn from each of business type and entrepreneurial venture, ultimately allowing you to develop an even better Rockstar Business model based on all of these influences. Through greater exposure to other industries and markets, you will be able to identify new gaps in various markets that you can potentially fill with your new ideas.

Most entrepreneurs would tell you that there is a lot of money to be made within niche needs and hobbies and that if you want to gain entry into those niches, you either need to do so with a unique, improved offering or by bringing a completely different angle to the table.

For Rockstars there is, however, an even bigger challenge: to find, discover or realize human behaviour upon which you can build a whole new niche. If you manage to create something outside of a preexisting niche box, you free yourself from the potential limitation and rules that already exist within popular and commonplace niches - you thus become the master of your own fate.

Developing a new niche will be one of the most difficult things to accomplish and not many of us will be successful in doing so. However, such outside-of-box thinking that goes along with this process will give you an immense advantage in formulating other and better ideas for existing niches as well. So, regardless of the outcome, the Rockstar wins either way.

Seemingly Ridiculous Ideas

When it comes to outside-the-box thinking and idea generating, a Rockstar may come up with some seemingly ridiculous ideas.

Before you discount the possibilities and potential that those represent, I would like to first ask you how many times you have looked at another business or idea and though to yourself, "Why didn't I think of that?"

That happens to all of us. Over and over again.

The only way to stop that trend is to actually pursue some of your own ridiculous ideas. Whilst they may seem completely stupid on the surface, there may be value (or an even better derivative idea) under that surface. I still don't believe that you should spend too much time exploring any idea - as your passion and gut-feel should already be an indicative measure - but don't just ignore an idea because it seems ridiculous, impossible or unprofitable.

95

If you decide to go after one of these "riskier" ideas, just do your-self one favour: limit your investment, in terms of your time and energy and especially your finances. Don't be caught with your pants around your ankles when it becomes apparent that the idea was just as ridiculous under the hood as it seemed when looking at it from the surface initially.

We produced a physical product called TypeFaces in early 2010, a set of "Web Designer Playing Cards," and was also a whole new ballgame for us. Previously, we had only worked on digital products and projects. But we wanted to try something that was unexpected from a "web design agency" and decided to have a go at manu-facturing a physical project.

The project wasn't a major success, but it has allowed the team to learn a bucket load about pursuing specific ideas going forward. Maybe the lack of significant suc-cess in this regard was due to the project being too much "out of the box" and thus not closely enough related to our core competency. However, the premise remains: just as much as an "out of box" idea can tank, it can also succeed in a spectacular fashion!

Be Vigilant

Rockstars ensure that they spend enough time outside of their own hype; that means getting out and getting yourself into potentially inspirational conversations and situations. Once again, as little as doing that can be the starting point to generate quite a few ideas. Nevertheless, it takes vigilance to generate the most viable and best ideas as often as possible.

Most people are too narrow-minded when it comes to inspiration and identifying potential gaps in markets (which are the probably the best starting points to use for any new idea). The trick is to not stress too much about the things around you, as that stress means you are only looking straight ahead and don't always see the inspiration and opportunities floating within your peripheral view.

If you are so focused on what you are doing at any given point in time, you will never be able to spot the many opportunities that almost fall in your lap every day. Be vigilant in your daily activities; ideas and inspiration are around you, and in abundance at that.

Do yourself a favour and don't ignore the possible Next-Big-Thing for the sake of stressing about today.

Working on similar projects within the same environment often means that it becomes a real challenge to be inspired by new potential business models and opportunities. If it does, try this fun little game that I play when I go shopping…

As I'm walking around shops or when I sit in a restaurant, I always try to think about their business model: how they are making their money, what kind of profit margin they expect on their products and services, and how they are aligning or positioning their brand and products. Whilst I obviously don't have any facts to back my assumptions (on most occasions anyway) since I don't have the intimate details or knowledge of their industry, the game is revitalizing in the way that it sparks my mind into action.

Ignore the Competition

Rockstars leave the "next move" choices to their competitors.

Deep competitor analysis is old school - mountains of inconclusive data is poison to unique ideas. Reactionary responses to what the other team is doing are not Rockstar.

Rockstars are not followers. We are proactive; we trust our own abilities and choices. We do not jeopardize our decisions by basing them on the actions of others or second-guessing other people's strategies. Pursuing a dream is risky and everyone has an opinion. Rockstars cut out unnecessary influences and trust their own minds.

This doesn't mean cutting out knowledge of the developments in the industry. Knowing what is going on is part of the game, but in the short term, outside changes shouldn't lead to a reactionary response or a sudden change in tactics.

Rockstars have a vision; we mindfully develop and tweak our processes to fit our goals, allowing for contingencies and taking into account the volatility of the market. Behaving in such a way allows us to predict important developments and be ahead of the pack: creating our unique strategies and adapting them to the bigger changes in our industry.

You would have picked it up by now that as a team, we at radiiate are more geared toward being unique than being profitable. The current incarnation of radiiate is not that of your average "web design and development agency," and for very good reason: we don't want to fit any mould and we don't want to do what our competition is doing. These reasons are why we decided to have a go at developing TypeFaces (a physical product) instead of simply exploring the possibilities of generating a passive income via a web or mobile app. I'm not suggesting that there's anything wrong with web or mobile apps (we'll probably also do this in future), but that's what the competition is doing already…

Balancing Contingencies

Many business theory guides will stress that a contingency plan is crucial in order to minimize risks if your original strategy does not come to fruition. I'm not going to argue with them. A "Plan B" is a pretty important thing to have in the vault and might save you if things don't go as you expected. More than that, ploughing on without a proper contingency plan is choosing to be blinded by arrogance, not becoming a Rockstar.

The biggest problem I see with contingency plans is that they can cause you to begin to doubt yourself. You may lose belief in yourself or your current strategies if you "need" to have a "Plan B." The fact of the matter is that a contingency is not called "Plan B" for nothing. It is your second choice. It isn't your "A" game. Do not invest significant time on formulating second, third or even fourth choice actions - put that energy and attention into your primary strategy.

To decide on a "Plan B" in a Rockstar kind of way, make the arrangements and then leave the details in a safe place. Shut the book, seal the envelope, lock the desk drawer… whatever you need to do to know that you are covered. You now have two strategies worthy of your interest (depending on what variables come into play), which leave you free to follow your primary and favoured option. You have established a balance between confidence in your own ideas and a get-out-of-jail card if stuff happens that means you need to make adjustments.

No Rockstar should be caught with their pants down. That would just be embarrassing.

"Plan A" with radiiate is to do as little as possible client work in favour of instead developing a passive income revenue model with either digital products and services or again exploring the possibility of augmenting our digital presence with physical by-products. So all of our energy and passion is aimed at Plan A, but client work (as a Plan B) is always on the table and a way of paying the bills and contributing to overheads whilst we develop revenue streams from Plan A.

Picking the right idea

We have established that generating a bunch of ideas is not the difficult part of building a Rockstar Business - actually picking the right idea to pursue is the tricky bit. Whilst there is no empirical evidence to suggest which ideas will work out the best, I'd like to suggest a few pointers and questions to ask that will help you pick the right idea:

#1 - Are you passionate about the idea? Moreover, what does your gut say about it? If the passion is there and your gut says jump at the opportunity, then that's a pretty clear indication that you will be able to succeed if the idea has legs within the context of your market or industry.

#2 - How unique is the idea? Does it try to solve a problem in an outside-the-box way? Both of these are great attributes for any new idea, as you are guaranteed that you won't initially have competition that uses a similar strategy to yours.

#3 - Have you considered as many avenues, industries as markets as possible? In addition, have you been vigilant in potentially identifying opportunities outside of the scope of your daily activities? These processes will give you a good idea of the potential out there, along with the context of picking the right idea (this especially helps if you need to decide between two great and seemingly equal ideas).

#4 - Is your idea based on plugging a gap within a market? If yes, you have a winning idea already, but you will still need to convince your target market that you are indeed plugging that cap in a valuable and cost-efficient way.

#5 - Looking at the financials, do you think this idea has legs? Can you fund it for long enough to build it out to the point where you can actually be profitable? If this looks overly risky in terms of financing and achieving positive cash flows, then you may be better advised to explore a different angle.

#6 - What does your landscape look like? What are your competitors doing? Your idea should never be overly influenced by your competitive environment, but sometimes it's not worth the risk to compete against a giant who owns 99% of the market you are trying to enter. You will need to consider each of these situations on merit, but sometimes it simply isn't worth the effort to battle that giant; irrespective of how great your idea may seem.

6.3 Running the Business (Model)

The day-to-day stuff

Build Something
Organic Growth
One Way Only - Add Value
Cash Flows, Financing and Wasting Money
Who's money to risk
Diversification and Sustainability
Checks and Balances

Build Something

You know exactly what a Rockstar's arsenal looks like: the attributes that you will need yourself, and the team and ideas that can potentially help to write your name into the business Hall of Fame. Irrespective of exactly what your arsenal looks like and what the ideas are that you have decided to pursue, you need to always have one, extremely important focus: build something that is bigger than yourself.

Most entrepreneurs make the mistake of associating themselves too closely with their businesses and ventures, which means that they never give those businesses the opportunity to run autonomously and independently from themselves. For Rockstars, this should be the ultimate goal. Enabling businesses to operate autonomously essentially frees up your own time to explore other avenues; meanwhile, the business continues to generate profits and builds your personal reputation.

The only way to achieve Rockstar Business autonomy is to build something that can operate and live on without you being involved in every process or activity. Some possibilities could take the form of a brand (this is generally the most obvious choice), a product or intellectual property. By combing the creation of those three elements into one company, you are building something of greater significance than your time and attention; doing so presents unlimited opportunity going forward.

Selling it on

The best way to put Rockstar Business autonomy into context would be to look at it from the angle of a potential buyer who is interested in purchasing something that you are building. Whilst a buyer would be interested to purchase your company based on its revenues and profits, they can't purchase it if there's nothing of value left after you extract yourself from the company.

What will a potential buyer be looking for? Assets are always a great starting point and this can take the shape of tangible assets (property) or intangible assets (your brand, the goodwill thereof and the possible intellectual property for your products). All of those things are valuable, even without your unique influence and control. Building something of value and something bigger than yourself should exist in your business.

To measure whether you are being successful in this regard, you can use the yardstick of portraying yourself as the potential buyer and new owner of your Rockstar Business. If you can see yourself purchasing the business, then you're on the right track.

> Back to bringing radiiate out of hibernation at the beginning of this year: When we were faced with the question of what we wanted to create, we could literally build any company that we wanted to build… We thus set out and spent a significant chunk of our time in laying out the groundwork of branding and the different channels that we wanted to move into, which became the basis of the new radiiate. We took these steps because we knew that as soon as we started to put different products, projects and services into place, the value of the company would be in the combination of the structure.
>
> We are building something - a company, a brand and many products - as you read this.

Build things up first

Have you ever noticed how impatient business owners are these days when it comes to growing and nurturing their businesses? Especially online… The modern impatient business model is all about developing some idea, get VC funding (or a massive loan from the bank), upgrade the office environment, hire a team of twenty employees (when they only need around five) and then splashing the rest of the cash on marketing. Sound familiar?

I've never subscribed to that kind of thinking. Whilst it isn't "wrong" per se, it definitely doesn't fit into my mindset of growing a business organically for as long as possible. In some cases, this approach may have merit, but in most situations, you would be challenged not to associate Rockstardom with organic growth.

The Right Way

Organic growth is all about pulling the trigger at the right moment, which will differ from person to person and business to business. The "right moment" will depend on a variety of factors, ranging from your personal level of comfort with the decision to the viability and sustainability of the decision from a profit-angle.

The main factor to consider, though, is the amount (and type) of work that needs to go into the business or project before you are able to pull the proverbial trigger.

During the initial stages of a project's lifespan, it's very easy to develop big parts of the idea using a D.I.Y. approach. During this stage, you take care of all the aspects of establishing the project - even though you may not be as great with some of the skills required (like admin or bookkeeping). Sometimes, you're going to need funds (VC or bank debt) to sustain the initial stages of the project, but even then there's a more conservative and organic way to approach financing.

The Rockstar Business approach allows you to invest time and money as you need it, which in turns means that you are already streamlining your growth. This is also a much more sustainable approach, as you're investing in further growth (because there is already traction for your project at that stage) instead of investing in overly ambitious, potential growth. I'm not saying don't invest in potential future growth, but I am warning you against overly ambitious investing.

Whilst the marketing-angle of any Rockstar will have an element of gung-ho risk-taking, it takes a better Rockstar to be conservative when they need to be. And then, it probably takes a perfect Rockstar to be able to pull that trigger at the perfect time in every situation - but that can only come with experience.

radiiate has been a business that has been in the works for a while now - and it obviously wasn't helped by the 10-month hibernation or the complete restructuring at the beginning of 2010. Prior to the hibernation, radiiate was starting to flourish as a boutique web design agency. However, when we moved the design and development team to WooThemes in the beginning of 2009, radiiate's growth took an inevitable backseat. Thus, when we relaunched the company in the beginning of 2010, we had the opportunity of starting from scratch.

The biggest thing you should take from my experience with radiiate is that whilst it would've been easier for me to invest truckloads of capital into radiiate to jumpstart the company into life, I instead opted to go back to the bootstrapping strategy that has worked so well for me before. Bootstrapping allowed me to build the company up organically from its roots. Although doing so means that radiiate is not a significant company yet, we're well on our way of growing it into one.

One Way Only: Add Value

There are many great business models out there - each with its own benefits and merits - but there is only one principle that is common every one of those models: If your company, products or services are adding value, then you are likely to succeed.

For you to earn a profit, someone needs to hand his or her hard-earned cash to you in return for what it is you are selling. The only rational reason for that person to spend their hard-earned money with you is if they perceive that transaction and exchange to hold value for them in some way or another.

You can delve into psychological pricing theories as much as you like, and you can have the most amazing of marketing campaigns that will convince people that your products or services are the only choice, but those will fail if you aren't rewarding each purchase with value.

In my mind, adding value is the only way that you can be semi-guaranteed that your business can be a success in the longer run. If your customers are only acting on irrational impulse when spending money with you, you'll soon see that trend fading - at which time, your only way of generating more revenue would be to move on to the next idea. Whilst possible, these methods aren't very sustainable or very Rockstar in the longer term.

Value your customers as well

Your customers are the lifeblood of your business; value them greatly. Similarly to ensuring that your products and services offer your customers significant value, you also need to ensure that you never threaten the trust relationship that exists between company and customer. If your customers feel like you have taken them for a ride, they won't be back spending more money with you in the future.

Valuing customers is especially critical considering that you are already vying for their attention in a crowded marketplace. Once you have them as your customers, it's important to offer continuous value and regular incentive to purchase more value from your company. A company with a loyal and happy customer-base is more likely to succeed in the long term - Rockstars make this one of their core focus areas.

We still work with friends and clients today that have been with us since the early days of radiiate. The reason for this? We have added as much value to our clients' experience as we possibly could, which in turn means they've become loyal supporters of the business.

Cash Flows, Financing & Wasting Money

At a very young age, a successful entrepreneur told me that a solid business would start showing an appropriate profit within two years of the opening of its doors. To this day, I still use that formula when evaluating new ideas: while there is no decisive or empirical evidence that suggests the theory to be unequivocally true, it has thus far been a safe measure.

With a 2-year timeframe, you need to evaluate whether you have sufficient financing to carry you for the duration of the two years that you have given yourself to reach profitability. The biggest concern isn't the fact that you need to be profitable (break-even would, for example, be fine as well), but that every startup needs to be cash flow positive. So many businesses ultimately fail not because they don't have a profitable or sustainable idea, but because they don't have cash at the right times and thus aren't able to continue paying their bills.

Rockstars need to manage finances conservatively and accurately and with the focus on being in control. I've always felt that as long as I knew exactly what was happening in my finances (either good or bad), I could back myself to find applicable short and long term solutions for potential issues that may arise.

Always know what your accounts look like and to give yourself enough space to find a solution if an emergency strikes: you need to ensure that you have enough funds in reserve to buy yourself some time.

Bootstrapping

The best way to give your finances a chance of surviving the startup phase is by proper bootstrapping across the board. By bootstrapping, I mean that you need to evaluate every cash outflow, irrespective of whether they are capital outlays or simply just expenditure. Don't waste money on things you really don't need.

Bootstrapping also means that you should only reinvest earnings into the business if you are relatively sure that it would lead to increases in your ultimate earnings. If not, then that cash has a better use just sitting in your bank account waiting for the day that you actually need it.

I'm not suggesting that you shouldn't allow yourself a few luxuries (as this is one of the benefits of being the boss!), but those should only make up a small percentage of your expenditure and it should never jeopardize the long term viability of your business. If buying yourself a new Mac means that you may not be able to pay office rent next month, then you probably shouldn't buy it.

If you bootstrap your Rockstar Business for long enough, you will eventually reach a level where you can spend more significant amounts of money without actually jeopardizing the business. Be patient initially and make sure that you bootstrap as much of Rockstar activities as possible.

Whose money to risk?

The subject of whose money should be risked in a Rockstar Business would appear to be a pretty easy question to answer, wouldn't it? Obviously, most business people would tell you to risk someone else's money than your own when pursuing (risky) ideas. That way, your personal wealth is unaffected should your new plans tank spectacularly, right? Wrong.

Within our existing corporate climate, we have so many great tools to assist budding entrepreneurs (and potential Rockstars) in attaining the finances that they need to pursue their business ideas. Venture capital, angel investors or seed investments are just some of the (relatively new) resources available to startup businesses. Whilst these offer undoubted value to future Rockstars, they should be considered beyond the obvious financial gain.

The bottom line is this: Rockstars don't risk others' money in a venture if they aren't willing to risk their own money as well.

It goes without saying that most startups simply don't have the financial means to finance a new operation. Allowing VCs or angel investors to invest and enable your ideas is a perfect way to eliminate the lack of funding - just remember that with the receipt of that investment, you also accept the responsibility to repay that investment.

If you don't truly believe in your idea (or, you only truly believe in an idea when you're willing to put your own money where your mouth is), don't take on the responsibility and risk that is packaged with the decision to take someone else's money.

Nobody is going to think of you as a true Rockstar if you're only gambling with other people's money.

I'm proud to have bootstrapped all of my investments, remaining wholly responsible for them myself. We have never taken outside funding or even considered taking bank debt. I have been lucky that we have been running cash flow positive from the beginning, which has most definitely made the bootstrapping process much easier. Nevertheless, it also means that I have had to take all the risk and the responsibility in justifying my business decisions by backing it up with my own money. Talk about putting your money where your mouth is, right?

Diversification & Sustainability

As soon as your new Rockstar Business is up-and-running and starting to generate proper profits at a nice rate of growth, you need to start focusing on turning your operations into a sustainable venture for the long term.

There are a few Rockstar methods to achieve sustainability (and with that desired long-term profitability), but the most obvious choice is a diversification of your interests. By diversifying interests and thus not putting all of your eggs in one basket, you are eliminating large chunks of the risk associated with running and owning a business.

The easiest way to achieve diversification is by reinvesting surplus funds in assets that generate a passive income. This is the most secure investment you can make and it creates a "Plan B" should your cash cow stop generating revenue. It is, however, also a very conservative decision and I don't know many Rockstars who will be overly happy to settle for only this avenue of diversification.

A Rockstar could also balance conservative, passive income with further reinvestment into new markets for your company. By launching new, semi-related projects within your business, you are creating new, potential revenue generating channels, which takes further pressure and risk away from your cash cow.

Don't multi-task, multi-project instead.

Rockstars are famous for their ability to multi-project and tap dance... but we'll save the tap dancing story for another day.

117

As Rockstars we are often involved with more than one project at the same time. The level of time and energy invested in each project will differ, Rockstars feel passionately about each and every one of them.

Old school conservatism advocates focusing on one project that utilises the individual's core competencies. There is absolutely nothing wrong with this approach; apart, of course, from the fact that it's not Rockstar at all!

A Rockstar attribute is our need for speed - we like things to happen quickly. We lose interest when life, projects and people don't move fast enough. One project is (in most cases) simply not enough to keep a us occupied. Multi-projecting is what keeps Rockstars sane and it distracts us from the destruction that accompanies boredom.

For Rockstars to effectively multi-project, there needs to be one main project - the sustainable business - consuming 80% of our working time. Here, it is business as usual, allowing the Rockstar to live life and meet responsibilities. The remaining 20% should consist of side-projects and reflect the Rockstar's interests and passions. It's this 20% that keeps the Rockstar refreshed, inspired, creative and a step ahead of the game.

We're most definitely not standing still at radiiate; we're multi-projecting as much as possible. We have a variety of irons in the fire, which is best evidenced by the different divisions within the company: iincubate, appliicate and fabriicate.

Our aim is to keep both our day-to-day tasks as fresh as possible, but also to diversify our revenue streams going forward. We believe that within this strategy we will find sustainability, which is the first goal. Thereafter? Profitability.

Checks & Balances

In the end, the life of your business remains firmly in your hands: if it fails, you will find that you are at least somewhat accountable for the reasons that led to the failure. Thus, as Rockstars it's important to implement appropriate checks and balances to make sure that you spot problems that may become critical down the line.

The first thing that you need to do is make sure that you know what's going on in your Rockstar Business - regardless of whether your company is just you, or you're a CEO with 500 employees beneath you. The buck stops with you. If you don't know what's going on in the company, then nobody else is going to take such a keen interest in it to identify potentially critical problems.

Whilst you are ensuring that you know what's happening, it's a great idea to continuously evaluate everything that is happening in your business. With each reevaluation, you are also able to tweak and possibly improve certain aspects thereof, which should streamline your efforts even further.

Evaluating and reevaluating is made much more difficult when everything in your Rockstar Business seems to be running smoothly and your profits appear to confirm the fact that you have indeed laid a golden egg. Nevertheless, you should always stay levelheaded and challenge your existing status quo - you would be making the biggest mistake of your business career if you start taking your success for granted.

Having the proper checks and balances in place will give you that firm basis from which you can continue to build your Rockstar Business (and hopefully, someday, turn it into a Rockstar Empire!).

I've learned the hard way that when things are going well for radiiate, I'm on top of the world. But when things aren't so great, I'm solely responsible and I stand alone in being accountable for that. This can come in the form of both criticism or a lack of financial success or viability. The key has been for me to take that on the chin and just move forward.

When I put the company into hibernation at the beginning of 2009 (to allow the team to join WooThemes and fuel our momentum there), I had to consider the investment that I had made into the company up until that point. For 10 months thereafter, we weren't doing anything that would earn a ROI (return on investment), and even when we started to rebuild the company in the beginning of 2010, the original investment still hadn't been fully justified. That's something that I've had to take on the chin, but fact of the matter is that we're working damn hard to make up for the hibernation period; the team has rallied around me and my vision to create something that will both be justified and significant in the long term.

7 | *Conclusion*

Conclusion

Although Rockstar Business has a lot to do with me - my personal outlook, beliefs about running a business and being an entrepreneur - the only reason that I wrote this book was for you, the reader, to find inspiration and adapt my Rockstar approaches, principles and their implementation to your life and your work in a uniquely "you" kind of way.

Being a Rockstar is not about mimicking Adii Rockstar, my entrepreneurial persona; or trying to emulate me, Adriaan Pienaar. Being a Rockstar is about you being you. You are a unique human being and no one will ever be quite like you - that, in itself, is a gift and the source of your motivation and empowerment. When you embrace and harness your passions, dedicate yourself to working harder than anyone else and embody a style of business leadership that is distinctively unlike the dying ways of the past, you're bound to discover some form of success.

Rockstar Business was not written by a global icon worth multiple billions who jets across the world on his every whim, stopping to lecture audiences of tens of thousands in between sightseeing ventures at each of the Wonders of the World. If it were, you would probably feel more satisfied and confident that copying my principles and business methods would work for you and without question.

However, that feeling of "guaranteed" success would merely be an illusion: trying to become someone else will only "guarantee" your ultimate failure.

In business, of course, success can never be guaranteed. Nevertheless, whether in your entrepreneurial ventures or in your daily life, I truly believe the wholesome and well-rounded principles I've espoused in Rockstar Business will help you achieve a greater sense of inner happiness, self-confidence and fulfillment. I can attest to those values because I am a living example of it, having found great inspiration, confidence and happiness in my young life. And, to the Rockstar, those kinds of successes are truly invaluable.

6102512R0

Made in the USA
Charleston, SC
14 September 2010